In the many letters I receive from friendly readers who have enjoyed my books, and feel compelled to tell me so, I have been struck by the number who have found in my writing just the right words which brought them comfort at a time when they needed it most.

It is not just the comedy which has impressed them, although readers seem to find identification with the hard but sometimes humorous side of poverty, and perceive the wisdom learned from my mother and my granny in maintaining self-respect and an independent spirit with little cash in the purse; it is also the description of bereavement, or deprivation, or sorrow, which has spoken to them most vividly. And so, because I feel that words do matter when we cannot find them for ourselves, I have been glad to be associated with these booklets whose contents have been chosen for their aptness for particular occasions.

I have selected pieces which have appealed most to myself and to others over the years, and I hope they will speak to your heart and mind when both need understanding and enrichment.

In this little book I have hoped to encourage a full warm appreciation of the joy and strength of the noon-day of the year and of our lives. So I have sought poems blending humour and challenge. All the actors to whom I have quoted Mrs Adlai Stevenson's advice to her son (page 26) have sighed enviously on hearing this counsel of perfection. It is truly splendid advice at all times of stress and uncertainty. It is only equalled by that other famous piece of philosophy: 'I have known many worries and fears in my life, most of which never happened!' Everything is possible if we rid ourselves of fear.

Molly Weir, 1987

Nor
love thy life
nor hate
But
whilst thou
livest
live well

Calligraphy by Louise Donaldson

A Birthday

My heart is like a singing bird
  Whose nest is in a watered shoot:
My heart is like an apple-tree
  Whose boughs are bent with thickest fruit;
My heart is like a rainbow shell
  That paddles in a halycon sea;
My heart is gladder than all these
  Because my love is come to me.

Raise me a daïs of silk and down:
  Hang it with vair and purple dyes;
Carve it in doves and pomegranates,
  And peacocks with a hundred eyes;
Work it in gold and silver grapes,
  In leaves and silver fleurs-de-lys;
Because the birthday of my life
  Is come, my love is come to me.

Christina Georgina Rossetti

Thairfore I say tae ye, be-na sair fashed wi care anent yer life; whit ye hae tae eat an whit ye hae tae drink. Nor yit for bodie; hoo ye are tae be cleedit. Isna the life mair nor mait, an the bodie mair nor cleedin? Luik ye tae the burds o the lift, for they naither saw nor reap, nor gaither intil barns; an yit yer Hevinlie Faither gies them fuid. Ye are wurth mair nor the burds.

Wha amang ye, wi grete worry, cuid mak hissel a span mair in heicht? An why fret aboot cleedin? Luik weel at the lilies o the field, hoo they graw; they toil-na nor spin, an yit I say that Solomon in aa his glorie wisna cleedit like ane o them. Noo than, gin God so cleeds the girse whilk graws the day an is cut doon in the morn, sall he no much mair cleed ye, o ye o smaa faith?

Yer Hevinlie Faither kens weel that ye need aa thae things, but seek ye firsten o aa God's reign an aa God's guidness, syne aa thae things will come tae ye as weel. Tak nae thocht anent the day tae come, for the morn will luik efter itsel. Ilka day has fash eneuch o its ain.

Jamie Stuart
Extract from *A Scots Gospel*

Upon A Child

Here a pretty baby lies
Sung asleep with lullabies.
Pray be silent and not stir
Th' easy earth that covers her.

Robert Herrick

A contented mind is a blessing kind
  and a merry heart is a purse well-lined,
So what care I, let the world go by,
For 'tis better far to laugh than cry!

Anon

Jenny Kiss'd Me

Jenny kiss'd me when we met,
  Jumping from the chair she sat in;
Time, you thief, who love to get
  Sweets into your list, put that in!
Say I'm weary, say I'm sad,
  Say that health and wealth have miss'd me,
Say I'm growing old, but add,
  Jenny kiss'd me.

Leigh Hunt

Lovely Things

Bread is a lovely thing to eat—
God bless the barley and the wheat!

A lovely thing to breathe is air—
God bless the sunshine everywhere!

The earth's a lovely place to know—
God bless the folks that come and go!

Alive's a lovely thing to be—
Giver of life—we say—bless Thee!

H M Sarson

Resolve not to be poor.
Whatever you have, spend less.
Poverty is a great enemy to human happiness.

Anon

Bredon Hill

In summertime on Bredon
The bells they sound so clear.
Round both the shires they ring them
    In steeples far and near
    A happy noise to hear.

Here of a Sunday morning
My love and I would lie,
And see the coloured counties,
    And hear the larks so high
    About us in the sky.

The bells would ring to call her
In valleys miles away;
'Come all to church, good people,
    Good people, come and pray'.
    But here my love would stay.

And I would turn and answer
Among the springing thyme,
'Oh peal upon our wedding,
    And we will hear the chime,
    And come to church in time'.

But when the snows at Christmas
On Bredon top were strown,
My love rose up so early
    And stole out unbeknown
    And went to church alone.

They tolled the one bell only,
Groom there was none to see,
And mourners followed after,
    And so to church went she,
    And would not wait for me.

The bells they sound on Bredon
And still the steeples hum.
'Come all to church, good people'—
    Oh noisy bells be dumb.
    I hear you, I will come.

A E Housman

Happiness is a mystery, like religion, and should never be rationalised.

G K Chesterton

Desiderata

Go placidly amid the noise and haste, and
remember what peace there may be in silence.
As far as possible without surrender be on good
terms with all persons. Speak your truth quietly
and clearly; and listen to others, even the dull
and ignorant; they too have their story.

Avoid loud and aggressive persons, they are
vexations to the spirit. If you compare yourself
with others, you may become vain and bitter;
for always there will be greater and lesser
persons than yourself. Enjoy your achievements
as well as your plans. Keep interested in your
own career, however humble; it is a real
possession in the changing fortunes of time.

Exercise caution in your business affairs; for
the world is full of trickery. But let this not
blind you to what virtue there is; many persons
strive for high ideals; and everywhere life is full
of heroism.

Be yourself. Especially do not feign affection.
Neither be cynical about love; for in the face of
all aridity and disenchantment it is perennial as
the grass.

Take kindly the counsel of the years,
gracefully surrendering the things of youth.
Nurture strength of spirit to shield you in
sudden misfortune. But do not distress yourself
with imaginings. Many fears are born of fatigue

and loneliness. Beyond a wholesome discipline, be gentle with yourself.

You are a child of the universe, no less than the trees and the stars. You have a right to be here. And whether or not it is clear to you, no doubt the universe is unfolding as it should. Therefore be at peace with God, whatever you conceive him to be, and whatever your labours and aspirations, in the noisy confusion of life keep peace with your soul.

With all its sham, drudgery and broken dreams, it is still a beautiful world.

Be careful.

Strive to be happy.

Inscribed on a gravestone in Old Saint Paul's Church, Baltimore, 1692

'*As one who jumps about like a fire-cracker from the moment I open my eyes in the morning, I have this piece framed, hanging in the bedroom, and I try to follow its excellent guidance. I haven't quite succeeded in achieving such perfection, but I'm still trying!*'

Whit will a man gain, altho he win the hale warld an tine his ain sowl?

Jamie Stuart
Extract from *A Scots Gospel*

Mary Hamilton

O Mary Hamilton to the kirk is gane
  Wi' ribbons in her hair;
An' the king thocht mair o' Marie
  Than onie that were there.

Mary Hamilton's to the preaching gane
  Wi' ribbons on her breast;
An' the king thocht mair o' Marie
  Than he thocht o' the priest.

Syne word is through the palace gane,
  I heard it tauld yestreen,
The king lo'es Mary Hamilton
  Mair than he lo'es the queen.

A sad tale through the town is gaen,
  A sad tale on the morrow:
Oh Mary Hamilton had born a babe
  And slain it in her sorrow.

And down then cam the auld queen,
  Goud tassels tied her hair:
'What did ye wi' the wee wee bairn
  That I heard greet sae sair?'

'There ne'er was a bairn into my room,
  An' as little designs to be;
'T was but a stitch o' my sair side
  Cam owre my fair bodie.'

'Rise up now, Marie', quo' the queen,
   'Rise up, an' come wi' me,
For we maun ride to Holyrood
   A gay wedding to see.'

The queen was drest in scarlet fine,
   Her maidens all in green;
An' every town that they cam through
   Took Marie for the queen.

But little wist Marie Hamilton
   As she rode owre the lea
That she was gaun to Edinbro' town
   Her doom to hear and dree.

When she cam to the Netherbow Port
   She laughed loud laughters three;
But when she reached the gallows-tree
   The tears blinded her e'e.

'Yestreen the queen had four Maries,
   The nicht she'll hae but three;
There's Marie Seaton, an' Marie Beaton,
   An' Marie Carmichael, an' me.

'Oh aften hae I dressed my queen
   An' put gowd in her hair;
The gallows-tree is my reward
   An' shame maun be my share.

'Oh aften hae I dressed my queen
   An' saft, saft made her bed;
An' now I've got for my reward
   The gallows-tree to tread.

'There's a health to all gallant sailors
   That sail upon the sea:
Oh never let on to my father and mither
   The death that I maun dee.

'An' I charge ye, all ye mariners,
   When ye sail owre the main,
Let neither my father nor mither know
   But that I'm comin hame.

'Oh little did my mither ken,
   That day she cradled me,
What lands I was to tread in
   Or what death I should dee.'

Anon

'*When I heard Celia read this ballad for the
"With Great Pleasure" programme, I was
particularly struck by the sly, slightly gossipy
tone she used, as one who is engaging some
scandal. It was so original and somehow just
right, and so I would like to use the same
version in this booklet. I am perhaps doubly
fortunate that I can hear her voice when I read
the lines.*'

M iracles sometimes occur,
But one has to work terribly hard for
them.

Weizmann

Summer Farm

Straws like tame lightnings lie about the grass
And hang zigzag on hedges. Green as glass
The water in the horse-trough shines.
Nine ducks go wobbling by in two straight lines.

A hen stares at nothing with one eye,
Then picks it up. Out of an empty sky
A swallow falls and, flickering through
The barn, dives up again into the dizzy blue.

I lie, not thinking, in the cool, soft grass,
Afraid of where a thought might take me—as
This grasshopper with plated face
Unfolds his legs and finds himself in space.

Self under self, a pile of selves I stand
Threaded on time, and with metaphysic hand
Lift the farm like a lid and see
Farm within farm, and in the centre, me.

Norman MacCaig

The Looking Glass And The Garden

This is my window; here I see
The self within my dazzled eyes.
To secret garden summoning me,
And thine its radiant skies.

Come soon, that twilight dusky hour,
When thou thyself shall enter in
And take my fill of every flower,
Since thine they've always been.

No rue? No Myrrh? No nightshade,
Oh! Tremble not spirit! All is well.
For Love is that lovely garden, and so
There only pleasures dwell.

Walter de la Mare

Mrs Adlai Stevenson's advice to her son—a thought to treasure.

Rid yourself of all fear. Fear of anything is absolutely devastating. It is the close relative of worry, the greatest waste of energy known—a simpleton's pastime.

Mrs Winston Churchill's philosophy—which I much admire and try to emulate.

Never enlarge upon your difficulties—except to tried and trusted friends.

Adlestrop

Yes. I remember Adlestrop—
The name, because one afternoon
Of heat the express-train drew up there
Unwontedly. It was late June.

The steam hissed. Someone cleared his throat.
No one left and no one came
On the bare platform. What I saw
Was Adlestrop—only the name.

And willows, willow-herb, and grass,
And meadowsweet, and haycocks dry,
No whit less still and lonely fair
Than the high cloudlets in the sky.

And for that minute a blackbird sang
Close by, and round him, mistier,
Farther and farther, all the birds
Of Oxfordshire and Gloucestershire.

Edward Thomas

The Quality Of Mercy

The quality of mercy is not strain'd,
It droppeth as the gentle rain from heaven
Upon the place beneath:
It is twice bless'd:
It blesseth him that gives, and him that takes:
'Tis mightiest in the mightiest; it becomes
The thronèd monarch better than his crown;
His sceptre shows the force of temporal power,
The attribute to awe and majesty,
Wherein doth sit the dread and fear of kings;
But mercy is above this sceptred sway,
It is enthronèd in the hearts of kings,
It is an attribute to God himself,
And earthly power doth then show likest God's
When mercy seasons justice.

William Shakespeare
Extract from *The Merchant of Venice*

God grant us the gifts of courage, gaiety,
and a quiet mind.

Anon

Acknowledgments

The Publishers gratefully acknowledge and thank the following for their kind permission to include copyright material in this booklet:

(Page 7) Published by Macmillan London Ltd; (8) Permission granted by Author; (12) 'Lovely Things' by H M Sarson from *Book of 100 Poems* (Unwin Hyman, London); (19) Permission granted by Author; (20-22) From *The Oxford Book of Ballads*, edited by James Kinsley (Oxford University Press, England, 1969); (24) 'Summer Farm' by Norman MacCaig, from *Collected Poems*. Permission granted by Author and Chatto & Windus, The Hogarth Press; (25) The Literary Trustees of Walter de la Mare and the Society of Authors as their representative; (29) 'Adlestrop' by Edward Thomas, courtesy of Faber & Faber Ltd, publishers of *Collected Poems* by Edward Thomas, and Myfanwy Thomas.

While every effort has been made to trace the holders of copyright, for some of the entries this has proved impossible. The Publishers would appreciate any relevant information which will ensure that acknowledgments omitted at this stage can be included in future editions.